This book belongs to:

_____

Illustrator: Rose Lyons

Editor: Rashell J. Campbell-Daughty, Ph.D.

Book Design: JaWaunn Glaze Sr.

ISBN: 978-0-578-83496-2

Published and Printed in the United States of American

Never Give Up

Written by: Chabli Glaze

Illustrated by Rose Lyons

DeShawn is excited about his new school and meeting new friends. He is a third-grader who likes to play basketball and baseball. Although DeShawn is nervous about who his teacher is, he wants to do his best at Campbell Elementary School. On the first day of school, while eating breakfast, DeShawn's mom reminds him of taking the beginning of the year test. She says, "DeShawn, I'm not sure when you will take the test, but when you do, I want you to do your very best."

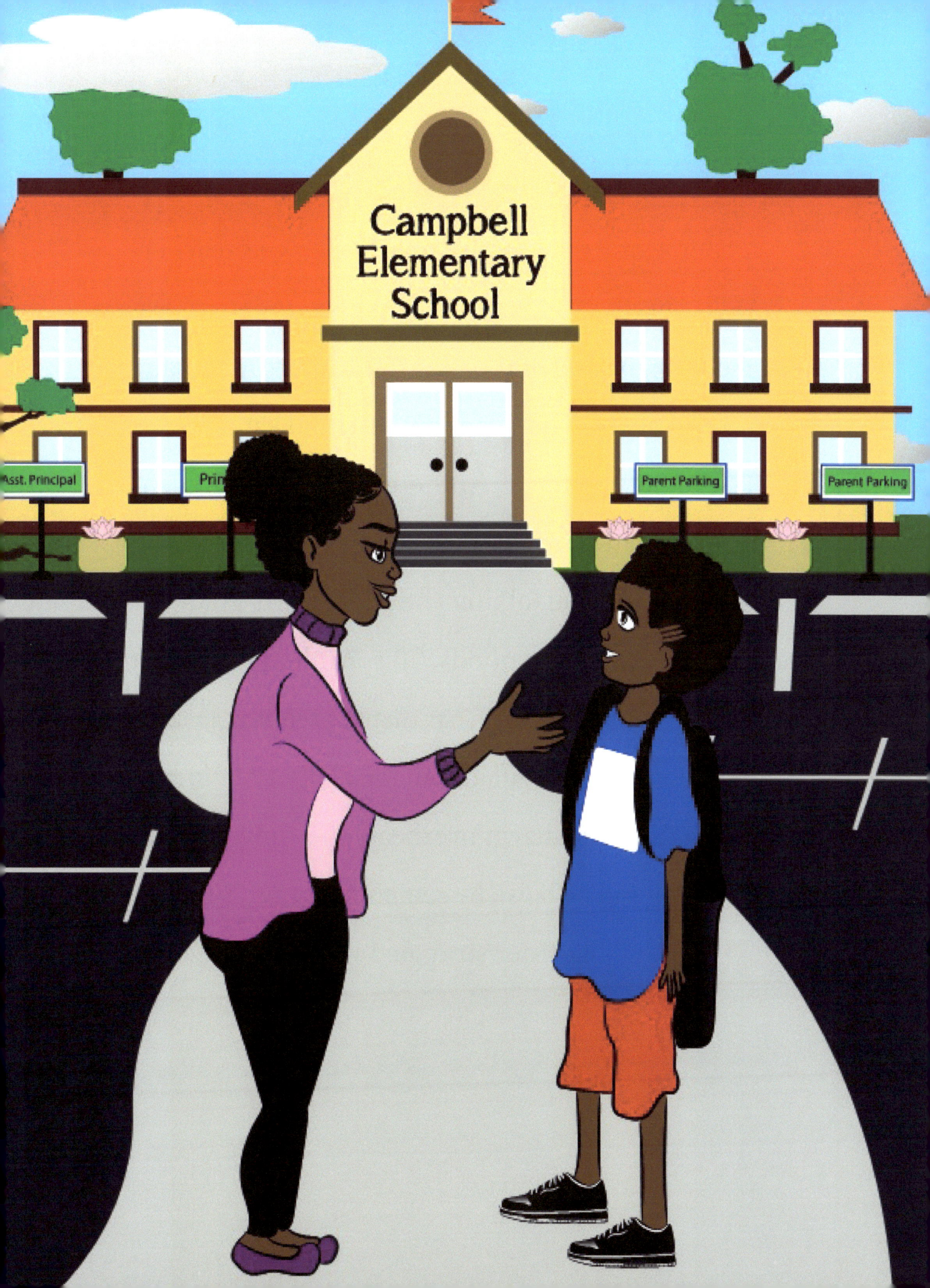

A couple of weeks pass by and DeShawn's teacher, Ms. Williams says, "Good morning boys and girls! We are taking our beginning of the year test tomorrow. I want you all to get in the bed, get plenty of rest, and eat a nutritious breakfast in the morning." Anthony, who is another student in DeShawn's class, raises his hand and says, "Ms. Williams, are you talking about the third-grade reading test?" Ms. Williams responds, "Yes, Anthony. This test is similar to your end-of-the-year district reading test. If you score high enough you will automatically be able to move on to fourth grade." DeShawn overhears the conversation and begins to look sad because he remembers that is the test his big sister struggled with.

After school, DeShawn goes home and shares with his parents about the upcoming test tomorrow. DeShawn says, "Mamma do you remember speaking to me about that test? Well, my teacher spoke to the whole class about it and she told us to get in the bed on time, get plenty of rest, and eat a nutritious breakfast in the morning." His Mom says, "I will make sure you get plenty of rest!" DeShawn's Dad says, "I will wake you and prepare breakfast in the morning ." DeShawn smiles and says," Thank you, Daddy!"

DeShawn awakes the next morning feeling nervous and insecure about the test and tells his parents about how he is feeling. His dad says, "You are very smart; don't worry." His mother says, "I will pray with you and give you some scriptures that will calm you." His mom prays with him and writes down the scripture: I can do all things through Christ who strengthens me Philippians 4:13. DeShawn smiles and says, "Thank you, Mamma." DeShawn takes the index card with the scripture and tapes it on the wall in his bedroom. Each time DeShawn walks past the index card, he reads the scripture.

The following morning, DeShawn awakes and heads to the kitchen and sees his dad cooking breakfast for the family. Dad says," Good Morning Deshawn. How did you sleep last night?"

"I slept good Daddy," says DeShawn. Mamma responds, "Glad to hear that you were able to rest!" DeShawn smiles and says, "Thank you Mamma for praying with me. I feel better now."

DeShawn goes to school and does his best while taking his test. Later that afternoon, before class dismissal, Ms. Williams gives every student an envelope. DeShawn gives his agenda and envelope to his mother. His mother opens the envelope and reads the letter. The letter shows DeShawn's scaled score of 200 and he needed 240 to pass.

DeShawn's mom shared the news with him and he cried. His Mom hugged him and told him that she would continue to help him more with his school work. While comforting him, his Mom reminded him of how dedicated and focused he is with baseball and basketball. She told DeShawn they were going to be equally focused with mastering the reading skills. Mom says, "The more you practice the better you will get."

Deshawn says, "Okay, Mamma."

Mom speaks to Ms. Williams about the next test date and Ms. Williams shares that the next test is in six weeks, so DeShawn begins reading every day for 40 minutes.

DeShawn is reading and Dad is asking story element questions.

Who are the characters? What is the setting? What is the problem?

What are the key events? What is the solution?

DeShawn is reading his book and Mom asks him to use the Venn diagram to compare and contrast the two characters.

Venn Diagram

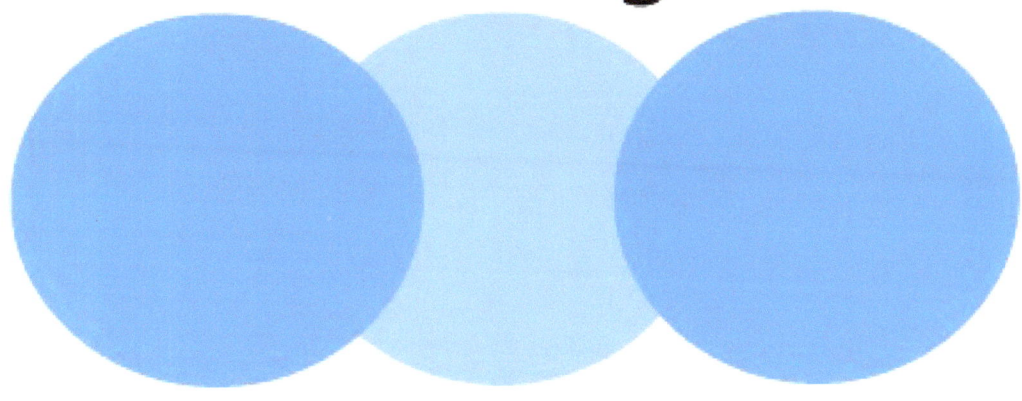

DeShawn is reading a new book and is asked to use the chart to fill in the sequence of events.

DeShawn is reading and Mom explains to him how to summarize a story.

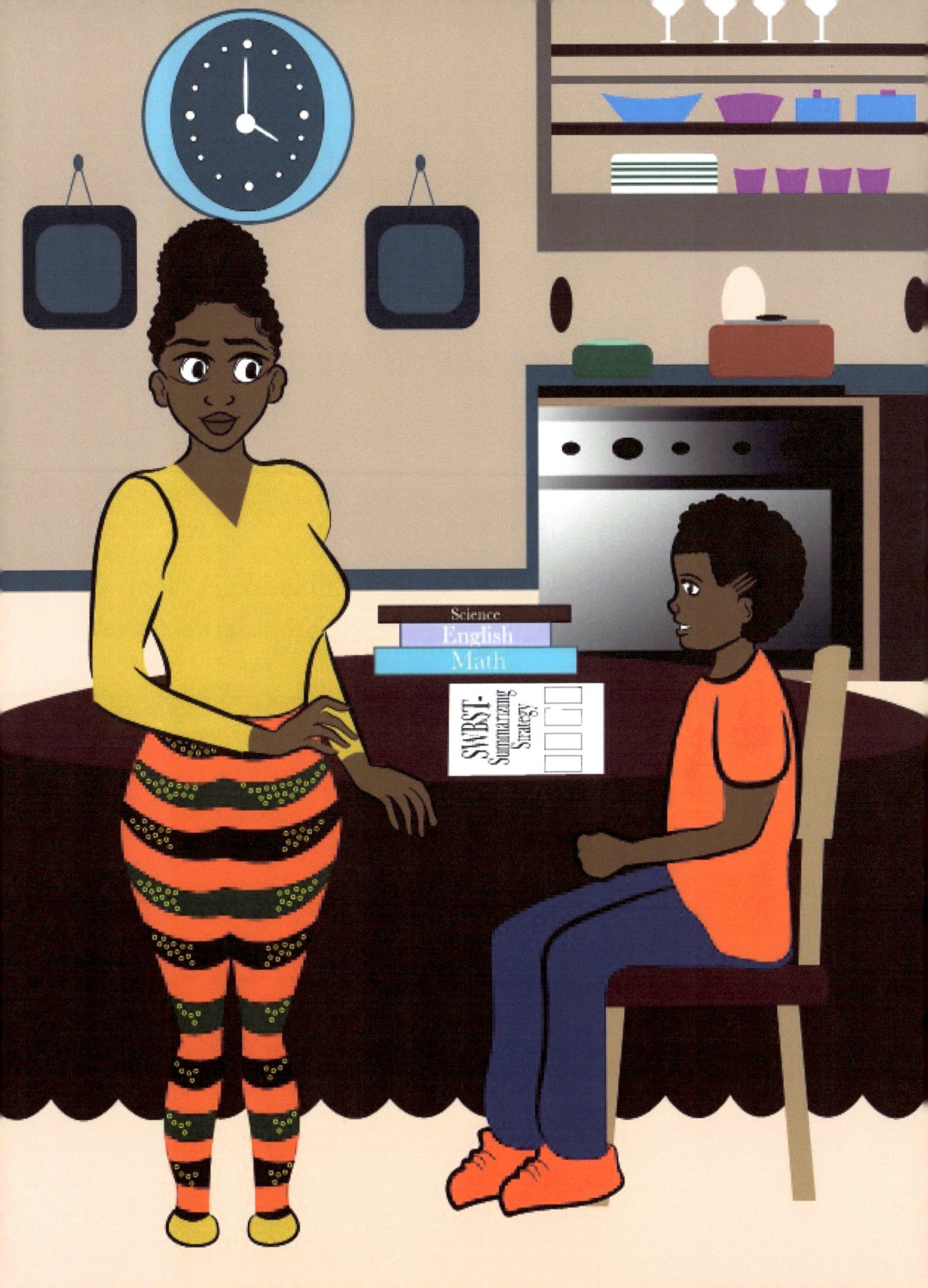

Ms. Williams says, "Boys and girls we have our next test before the holiday break which is Monday. Remember to get plenty of rest, and eat a nutritious breakfast!"

On the morning of the test, DeShawn awakes and is ready to have breakfast with his family. His Mom asks, "DeShawn are you ready for your test?" DeShawn responds, "Yes ma'am! We have practiced on my reading skills for six weeks, and I am ready to take the test!" After getting into the car, DeShawn asks his mother, "Can we pray before I go to school?" Soon after, Mom says a prayer for DeShawn and drops him off at school.

DeShawn walks into his classroom and has a seat at his desk. He is excited and ready for his test. Ms. Williams says," Good Morning boys and girls! Before we begin our test, I am going to pass out an envelope to each student and I want you to read the note inside. When you have read the note, put it inside your desk, and I will give you your test." DeShawn reads his mother's note silently and smiles. He put the note inside his desk and begins the test. Before the end of the day dismissal, Ms. Williams passes out the test result envelope to each student.

Son, you've got this!
You have worked
hard and remember
to do your best!
I can do all things
through Christ that
strengtheneth me.
Phil. 4:13
Love Mom

DeShawn goes home and gives the envelope to his mom. His mom opens the envelope and reads the letter. It says that DeShawn passed the test with a score of 260. Mom says, "DeShawn, guess what? You passed your test! You did it, DeShawn!" At that moment, DeShawn realized that all of his hard work paid off.

The family celebrated DeShawn's accomplishment with a family fun day. They enjoyed ice cream and games at the local park. It was a great day and DeShawn learned to "Never Give Up."

About the Author

Chabli Glaze is a Spencer, Oklahoma native who earned her Master's Degree in Special Education. As an Educator and business owner of Academic Elevation Tutoring, she quickly identified the skills that were lacking in her community and decided to return to her humble beginnings to transform the lives of current students. Mrs.Glaze is a wife and mother of four beautiful children who enjoys spending time with her family and friends.